CHINESE Spice
RECIPES

PARRAGON

CHINESE *Spice*

RECIPES

Exotic Dishes Flavoured with Spices

First published in Great Britain in 1996 by
Parragon Book Service Ltd
Unit 13-17, Avonbridge Trading Estate
Atlantic Road, Avonmouth
Bristol BS11 9QD

ISBN: 0-7525-1973-5

Printed in the United Kingdom

Produced by Kingfisher Design, London

Acknowledgements
Series Design: Pedro Prá-Lopez, Kingfisher Design, London
Designers: Frank Landamore, Frances Prá-Lopez, Kingfisher Design, London
Series Editor: Diana Vowles
Illustrations: Jill Moore
Photography: Amanda Heywood, Joff Lee
Home Economists: Deh-Ta Hsiung, Wendy Lee
Stylists: John Lee Studios, Marian Price

Material contained in this book has previously appeared in
Chinese Cantonese Cooking, Vegetarian Chinese Cooking and
Chinese Szechuan Cooking

Note
Cup measurements in this book are for American cups.
Tablespoons are assumed to be 15ml.
Unless otherwise stated, milk is assumed to be full-fat,
eggs are standard size 2 and pepper is freshly ground black pepper

Contents

Chinese Cooking

Chinese cooking is one of the oldest cuisines in the world, and it differs from all others in that it is based on a philosophy of balancing harmony and contrast following the yin-yang principles of traditional Chinese cosmology. While it is divided into four different regional styles – Cantonese, Shanghai, Szechuan and Peking – these principles apply throughout, and to every dish as well as the meal as a whole. However, the Chinese have exported their cuisine throughout the world and the majority of Western diners enjoy it purely for its flavours without feeling the need to understand the philosophies that lie behind it. The same applies to Western cooks; while the recipes in this book have been designed for harmony of flavour, colour and texture, all you need to do is enjoy cooking and eating them!

The daily diet of the average Chinese is based largely on rice, vegetables and fresh noodles, with fish and meat added in small quantities to give flavour. Dairy products are not used at all. Consequently, now that scientists have discovered the disadvantages to health caused by eating animal fats, the Chinese diet is regarded one of the healthiest in the world.

The staples of Chinese food

Chinese food relies on a relatively small number of spices, the main ones being chilli, sesame and five-spice powder. Chillies, though they originated in South and Central America and the West Indies rather than in China, feature heavily in a number of variations: fresh and dried chillies, chilli powder, chilli oil and chilli bean sauce all add a dash of heat to a Chinese dish, and strips of fresh chilli act as a typically delicate garnish. China is now the

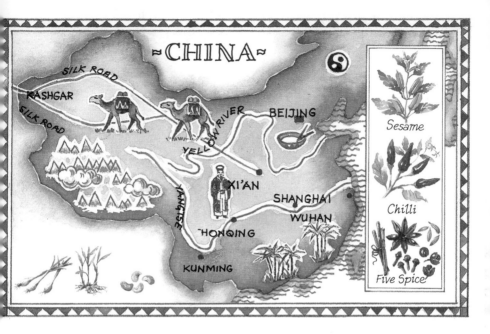

rgest producer of chillies in the world. Sesame also appears in many dishes, hough it is most often used in the form f sesame oil, acting as a garnish rather han as a cooking medium. It is believed o be the oldest plant grown for oil, and was certainly in use for its medicinal ualities in Egypt in about 1550BC. Its rigin is obscure, though Africa, Iran, ndia and Indonesia have been suggested nd it was known in China 2000 years go. Today it is mainly grown in China,

India, Mexico, Central America and the southwest United States.

Sesamum indicum is an annual plant that grows up to about 1.5 m/5 ft, with oval leaves and white or pink bell-shaped flowers. Harvesting takes place when the seedpods at the top of the plants are still green. The plants are then threshed and dried and the seed is sold as it is or processed into oil, being toasted first to make the dark, nutty Oriental variety. The seeds may be white, brown or black, the white variety being most common and mildest in flavour.

The complete spice

Five-spice is probably the most famous Chinese flavouring. The basic mix is of star anise, Szechuan peppercorns, fennel seeds, cinnamon or cassia and cloves, though cardamom, ginger and liquorice may be added as well. Five-spice powder is highly pungent and should be used sparingly. It varies from brown to amber and the liquorice flavour of star anise predominates. This spice, native to China and Vietnam, comes from an evergreen tree, *Illicium verum*, related to magnolia. The star-shaped fruits are picked before they ripen and dried in the sun.

Szechuan peppercorns come from a tree called *Xanthoxylum piperitum* and are not related to the peppercorns we use daily, which are from the *Piper* genus. Variously called fagara, farchiew and Chinese pepper among other names,

Szechuan peppercorns are reddish-brown dried berries with a prickly exterior. *Xanthoxylum piperitum* grows wild throughout China and its berries have been used there since ancient times.

Fennel *(Foeniculum vulgare)* is a native of the Mediterranean, though it is naturalized in many temperate countries. It is related to caraway, anise and dill and shares their familiar liquorice-like flavour.

Cinnamon is another spice familiar in the West. It is the bark of *Cinnamomum verum*, a tree native to Sri Lanka but now grown in Brazil, the West India, India, Indonesia and islands of the Indian Ocean. The branches are cut in the rainy season and the bark is stripped off and dried for 24 hours. The exterior layer is then removed, leaving the inside to be handrolled into quills which are dried in the shade, taking on their warm brown colour in the process. Cassia comes from *Cinnamomum cassia*, a related tree which grows in the Far East. It is often used instead of cinnamon, though it has a more intense, less delicate flavour.

The great prize

Cloves, the fifth spice, are the flower buds of *Eugenia caryophyllata*, a tree from the Moluccas (formerly the Spice Islands) in the Indian Ocean. Of ancient use in China, they gradually became known in Europe, where they were so prized that in the 16th century the Dutch seized the Spice Islands from the Portuguese to gain control of the clove trade. They limited cultivation to just one island to protect their monopoly, but the attempt failed – in the 18th century the French smuggled seedlings to Mauritius and in the 19th century the British East India Company sent trees to India, Sri Lanka and Kew Gardens in the UK. Today, this much fought-over spice is produced in Indonesia, Tanzania, Sri Lanka and Grenada in the West Indies.

So the five-spice powder that we use today almost provides a history of the whole spice trade, with its travels and its trading, its wars and its subterfuge. Fortunately, all we need do is shake it into the wok!

Chinese Stock

A basic stock is much used in Chinese cooking, not only as the basis for soup-making but also whenever liquid is required instead of plain water. Since the amounts required are sometimes small, it makes sense to freeze it in mini-containers and defrost as required.

MAKES 2.5 LITRES/4 PT/10 CUPS

750 g /1½ lb chicken pieces
750 g /1½ lb pork spare ribs
3.75 litres /6 pints /15 cups cold water
3–4 pieces ginger root, crushed
3–4 spring onions (scallions), each tied into a knot
3–4 tbsp Chinese rice wine or dry sherry

1 Trim off excess fat from the chicken and spare ribs, then chop them into large pieces.

2 Place the chicken and pork in a large pan with water and add the ginger and spring onion (scallion) knots. Bring to the boil and skim off the scum. Reduce the heat and simmer uncovered for at least 2–3 hours.

3 Strain the stock, discarding the chicken, pork, ginger and spring onions (scallions); add the wine and return to the boil, then simmer for 2–3 minutes. Refrigerate the stock when cool; it will keep for up to 4–5 days.

Deep-fried Prawns (Shrimp) with Spicy Salt and Pepper

SERVES 4

250–300 g / 8–10 oz uncooked tiger
prawns (jumbo shrimp) in their shells,
defrosted if frozen
1 tbsp light soy sauce
1 tsp Chinese rice wine or dry sherry
2 tsp cornflour (cornstarch)
vegetable oil, for deep-frying
2–3 spring onions (scallions), cut into short
sections, to garnish

SPICY SALT AND PEPPER:
1 tbsp salt
1 tsp ground Szechuan peppercorns
1 tsp five-spice powder

1 Pull the soft legs off the prawns
(shrimp), but keep the body shell on.
Dry well on paper towels.

2 Place the prawns (shrimp) in a bowl
with the soy sauce, wine and cornflour
(cornstarch). Turn until well coated and
leave to marinate for 25–30 minutes.

3 To make the Spicy Salt and Pepper,
mix the salt, pepper and five-spice
powder together. Place in a dry frying pan
(skillet) and stir-fry for about 3–4 minutes
over a low heat, stirring constantly.
Remove from the heat and allow to cool.

4 Heat the oil in a preheated wok or
large frying pan (skillet) until smoking,
then deep-fry the prawns (shrimp) in
batches until golden brown. Remove the
prawns (shrimp) with a slotted spoon and
drain on paper towels.

5 Place the spring onions (scallions) in a
bowl, pour on 1 tablespoon of the hot
oil and leave for 30 seconds. Serve the
prawns (shrimp) garnished with the spring
onions (scallions), and with Spicy Salt and
Pepper as a dip.

Tofu (Bean Curd) Sandwiches

MAKES 28

4 Chinese dried mushrooms (if unavailable,
   use thinly sliced open-cup mushrooms)
275 g / 9 oz tofu (bean curd)
½ cucumber, grated
1 cm / ½ inch piece ginger root, grated
60 g / 2 oz / ¼ cup cream cheese
salt and pepper

BATTER:
125 g / 4 oz / 1 cup plain (all-purpose)
   flour
1 egg, beaten
120 ml / 4 fl oz / ½ cup water
½ tsp salt
2 tbsp sesame seeds
vegetable oil for deep-frying

SAUCE:
150 ml / ¼ pint / ⅔ cup natural yogurt
2 tsp honey
2 tbsp chopped fresh mint

1 Place the dried mushrooms in a bowl
and cover with warm water. Leave to
soak for 20–25 minutes. Drain and
squeeze out the excess water. Remove the
tough centres and chop the mushrooms.

2 Drain the tofu (bean curd) and slice
thinly, then cut each slice to make
2.5 cm/1 inch squares.

3 Squeeze the excess liquid from the
cucumber and mix the cucumber with
the mushrooms, ginger and cream cheese.
Season well. Use as a filling to sandwich
slices of tofu (bean curd) together to
make about 28 sandwiches.

4 To make the batter, sift the flour into a
bowl. Beat in the egg, water and salt
to make a thick batter. Stir in the sesame
seeds. Heat the oil in a preheated wok or
large saucepan. Coat the sandwiches in
the batter and deep-fry in batches until
golden. Remove with a slotted spoon and
drain on paper towels.

5 To make the dipping sauce, blend
together the yogurt, honey and
mint. Serve the sauce with the tofu (bean
curd) sandwiches.

Bang-Bang Chicken

SERVES 4

1 litre / 1¾ pints / 4⅓ cups water
2 chicken quarters (breast half and leg)
1 cucumber, cut into matchstick shreds

SAUCE:
2 tbsp light soy sauce
1 tsp sugar
1 tbsp finely chopped spring onions
*   (scallions)*
1 tsp red chilli oil
¼ tsp pepper
1 tsp white sesame seeds
2 tbsp peanut butter, creamed with a little
* ᵒ sesame oil*

1 Bring the water to a rolling boil in a wok or a large saucepan. Add the chicken pieces, reduce the heat, cover and cook for 30–35 minutes.

2 Remove the chicken from the wok or pan and immerse it in a bowl of cold water for at least 1 hour to cool it.

3 Remove the chicken pieces and drain well. Dry on paper towels, then take the meat off the bone.

4 On a flat surface, pound the chicken with a rolling pin, then tear the meat into shreds with your fingers or with 2 forks. Mix with the shredded cucumber and arrange in a serving dish.

5 To serve, mix together all the sauce ingredients and pour over the chicken and cucumber.

Deep-fried Spare Ribs

SERVES 4

8–10 spare ribs
salt and pepper
1 tsp five-spice powder or 1 tbsp mild curry
    powder
1 tbsp rice wine or dry sherry
1 egg
2 tbsp plain (all-purpose) flour
vegetable oil for deep-frying
1 tsp finely shredded spring onions
    (scallions)
1 tsp finely shredded fresh green or red hot
    chillies
Spicy Salt and Pepper (see page 10), to serve

1 Chop the ribs into 3–4 small pieces.
Place the ribs in a bowl with salt,
pepper, five-spice or curry powder and
the wine or sherry. Turn to coat the ribs in
the spices and leave them to marinate for
1–2 hours.

2 Mix the egg and flour together to
make a batter.

3 Dip the ribs in the batter one by one
to coat well.

4 Heat the oil in a preheated wok or
large frying pan (skillet) until smoking.
Deep-fry the ribs for 4–5 minutes, then
remove with a slotted spoon and drain on
paper towels.

5 Reheat the oil over a high heat and
deep-fry the ribs once more for a
further minute. Remove and drain again
on paper towels.

6 Pour 1 tablespoon of the hot oil over
the spring onions (scallions) and
chillies and leave for 30–40 seconds.
Serve the ribs with Spicy Salt and Pepper,
garnished with the shredded spring
onions (scallions) and chillies.

Barbecue Pork (Char Siu)

SERVES 4

500 g / 1 lb pork fillet (tenderloin)
150 ml / ¼ pint / ⅔ cup boiling water
1 tbsp honey, dissolved with a little hot water
shredded lettuce to serve

MARINADE:
1 tbsp sugar
1 tbsp crushed yellow bean sauce
1 tbsp light soy sauce
1 tbsp hoi-sin sauce
1 tbsp oyster sauce
½ tsp chilli sauce
1 tbsp brandy or rum
1 tsp sesame oil

1 Cut the pork into strips about 2.5 cm/1 inch thick and 18–20 cm/ 7–8 inches long and place in a large shallow dish. Add the marinade ingredients and turn the pork until well coated. Cover and leave to marinate for at least 3–4 hours, turning occasionally.

2 Preheat the oven to 220°C/425°F/Gas mark 7. Remove the pork strips from the dish with a slotted spoon, reserving the marinade to use for basting. Arrange the pork strips on a rack over a baking tin (pan). Place the tin (pan) in the oven and pour in the boiling water. Roast for about 10–15 minutes.

3 Lower the oven temperature to 180°C/350°F/Gas mark 4. Baste the pork strips with the reserved marinade and turn. Roast for a further 10 minutes.

4 Remove the pork from the oven, brush with the honey syrup and place under a medium-hot grill (broiler) for 3–4 minutes or until lightly brown, turning once or twice.

5 To serve, allow the pork to cool slightly before cutting it. Cut across the grain into thin slices and arrange on a bed of shredded lettuce. Make a sauce by boiling the marinade and the drippings in the baking tin (pan) for a few minutes, then strain it and pour it over the pork.

Sweetcorn (Corn) & Lentil Soup

SERVES 4

30 g / 1 oz / 2 tbsp green lentils
1 litre / 1¾ pints / 4⅓ cups vegetable stock
1 cm / ½ inch piece ginger root, chopped finely
2 tsp soy sauce
1 tsp sugar
1 tbsp cornflour (cornstarch)
3 tbsp dry sherry
325 g / 11 oz can sweetcorn (corn)
1 egg white
1 tsp sesame oil
salt and pepper

TO GARNISH:
strips of spring onion (scallion)
strips of red chilli

1 Wash the lentils in a sieve (strainer). Place in a wok or saucepan with the stock, ginger, soy sauce and sugar. Bring to the boil and boil rapidly, uncovered, for 10 minutes. Skim off any froth on the surface. Reduce the heat, cover and simmer for 15 minutes.

2 Mix the cornflour (cornstarch) with the sherry in a small bowl. Add the sweetcorn (corn) with the liquid from the can and the cornflour (cornstarch) mix to the wok or saucepan. Simmer over a low heat for 2 minutes, stirring occasionally.

3 Whisk the egg white lightly with the sesame oil. Pour the egg mixture into the soup in a thin stream, remove from the heat and stir. The egg white will form white strands.

4 Season the soup to taste with salt and pepper. Pour into 4 warmed soup bowls and garnish with strips of spring onion (scallion) and chilli before serving.

CANNED LENTILS

To save time, you can use a 425 g / 14 oz can of green lentils. Place in a wok or saucepan with the stock and flavourings, simmer for 2 minutes, then continue the recipe from step 2 as above.

Lettuce & Tofu
(Bean Curd) Soup

SERVES 4

200 g / 7 oz tofu (bean curd)
2 tbsp vegetable oil
1 carrot, sliced thinly
1 cm / ½ inch piece ginger root, cut into
   thin shreds
3 spring onions (scallions), sliced diagonally
1.25 litres / 2 pints / 5 cups vegetable stock
2 tbsp soy sauce
2 tbsp dry sherry
1 tsp sugar
125 g / 4 oz / 1½ cups cos (romaine)
   lettuce, shredded
salt and pepper

1 Cut the tofu (bean curd) into small cubes. Heat the oil in a preheated wok or large saucepan, add the tofu (bean curd) and stir-fry until browned. Remove with a slotted spoon and drain on paper towels.

2 Add the carrot, ginger and spring onions (scallions) to the wok or saucepan and stir-fry for 2 minutes.

3 Add the stock, soy sauce, sherry and sugar. Bring to the boil and simmer for 1 minute.

4 Add the lettuce and stir until it has just wilted.

5 Return the tofu (bean curd) to the wok or saucepan to reheat. Season to taste with salt and pepper and serve in warmed bowls.

Sweetcorn (Corn) & Crab Meat Soup

SERVES 4

125 g / 4 oz crab meat
¼ tsp finely chopped ginger root
2 egg whites
2 tbsp milk
1 tbsp cornflour (cornstarch) paste (see page 30)
600 ml / 1 pint / 2½ cups Chinese Stock (see page 9)
250 g / 8 oz can American-style creamed sweetcorn (corn)
salt and pepper
finely chopped spring onions (scallions), to garnish

1 Flake the crab meat and mix with the ginger.

2 Beat the egg whites until frothy, add the milk and cornflour (cornstarch) paste and beat again until smooth. Blend in the crab meat.

3 In a wok or large saucepan, bring the stock to the boil. Add the creamed sweetcorn (corn) and bring the mixture back to the boil.

4 Stir in the crab meat and egg-white mixture, adjust the seasoning and stir gently until the mixture is well blended. Serve hot, garnished with chopped spring onions (scallions).

CREAMED CORN

Although sweetcorn (corn) is not unknown in Asia today, it really is a Western food by tradition. Be sure to use proper creamed sweetcorn (corn) for this soup, as it has quite a different texture from the more usual sweetcorn (corn) kernels. Creamed sweetcorn (corn) has a thick, slightly mushy consistency, making a thick, creamy soup.

Fish with Black Bean Sauce

SERVES 4–6

1 sea bass, trout or turbot, weighing about
*   750 g / 1½ lb, cleaned*
1 tsp salt
1 tbsp sesame oil
2–3 spring onions (scallions), cut in half
*   lengthways*
1 tbsp light soy sauce
1 tbsp Chinese rice wine or dry sherry
1 tbsp finely shredded ginger root
1 tbsp oil
2 tbsp crushed black bean sauce
2 spring onions (scallions), finely shredded

TO GARNISH:
sprigs of fresh coriander (cilantro) (optional)
lemon slices

1 Score both sides of the fish with
diagonal cuts at 2.5 cm/1 inch
intervals. Rub both the inside and outside
of the fish with salt and sesame oil.

2 Place the fish on top of the spring
onions (scallions) on a heat-proof
platter. Blend the soy sauce and wine or
sherry with the ginger shreds and pour
evenly all over the fish.

3 Place the fish on the platter in a very
hot steamer (or inside a wok on a
rack), cover and steam vigorously
for 12–15 minutes or until the flesh
flakes easily.

4 Heat the oil until hot, then blend in
the black bean sauce. Remove the fish
from the steamer and place on a serving
dish. Pour the hot black bean sauce over
the whole length of the fish and place the
shredded spring onions (scallions) on top.

5 Serve garnished with sprigs of
coriander (cilantro) and lemon slices.

FISH STEAKS

*If using fish steaks, rub them with the salt and
sesame oil, but do not score with a knife. The
fish may require less cooking, depending on
the thickness of the steaks; test for doneness
with a skewer after about 8 minutes.*

Crab with Ginger

SERVES 4

1 large or 2 medium crabs, weighing about
   750 g / 1½ lb in total
2 tbsp Chinese rice wine or dry sherry
1 egg, lightly beaten
1 tbsp cornflour (cornstarch)
3–4 tbsp vegetable oil
1 tbsp finely chopped ginger root
3–4 spring onions (scallions), cut into
   sections
2 tbsp light soy sauce
1 tsp sugar
about 75 ml / 2½ fl oz / 5 tbsp Chinese
   Stock (see page 9) or water
½ tsp sesame oil
sprigs of coriander (cilantro) to garnish

1 Cut the crab in half from the under-belly. Break off the claws and crack them with the back of a cleaver or a large kitchen knife.

2 Discard the legs and crack the shell, breaking it into several pieces. Discard the feathery gills and the stomach sac. Place in a bowl with the wine or sherry, egg and cornflour (cornstarch) and leave to marinate for 10–15 minutes.

3 Heat the oil in a preheated wok or large frying pan (skillet) and stir-fry the crab with the ginger and spring onions (scallions) for 2–3 minutes.

4 Add the soy sauce, sugar and stock or water, blend well and bring to the boil. Cover and cook for 3–4 minutes, then remove the cover, sprinkle with sesame oil and serve, garnished with sprigs of coriander (cilantro).

Stir-fried Prawns (Shrimp)

SERVES 4

170 g / 6 oz uncooked prawns (shrimp), peeled
1 tsp salt
¼ tsp egg white
2 tsp cornflour (cornstarch) paste (see below)
300 ml / ½ pint / 1¼ cups vegetable oil
1 spring onion (scallion), cut into short sections
2.5 cm / 1 inch piece ginger root, sliced thinly
1 small green (bell) pepper, cored, deseeded and cubed
½ tsp sugar
1 tbsp light soy sauce
1 tsp rice wine or dry sherry
a few drops of sesame oil

1 Mix the prawns (shrimp) with a pinch of the salt, the egg white and the cornflour (cornstarch) paste until they are all well coated.

2 Heat the oil in a preheated wok or large frying pan (skillet) and stir-fry the prawns (shrimp) for 30–40 seconds only. Remove and drain on paper towels.

3 Pour off the oil, leaving about 1 tablespoon in the wok or frying pan (skillet). Add the spring onion (scallion) and ginger to flavour the oil for a few seconds, then add the green (bell) pepper and stir-fry for about 1 minute.

4 Add the remaining salt and the sugar, followed by the prawns (shrimp). Continue stirring for another minute or so, then add the soy sauce and wine or sherry and blend well. Sprinkle with sesame oil and serve immediately.

CORNFLOUR (CORNSTARCH) PASTE

Cornflour (cornstarch) paste is made by mixing 1 part cornflour (cornstarch) with about 1½ parts cold water. Stir until smooth.

Fried Squid Flowers

*350–400 g / 12–14 oz prepared and
cleaned squid (see below right)*
*1 medium green (bell) pepper, cored and
deseeded*
3–4 tbsp vegetable oil
1 garlic clove, chopped finely
¼ tsp finely chopped ginger root
*2 tsp finely chopped spring onions
(scallions)*
½ tsp salt
2 tbsp crushed black bean sauce
1 tsp Chinese rice wine or dry sherry
a few drops of sesame oil

1 If the squid is not ready-prepared,
prepare and clean it as instructed.

2 Open up the body of the squid and
score the inside of the flesh in a
criss-cross pattern using a cleaver or
kitchen knife.

3 Cut the body and tentacles of the
squid into pieces of about 3 cm/
1½ inches in size. Blanch in a bowl of
boiling water for a few seconds. Remove
and drain, then dry well on paper towels.

4 Cut the (bell) pepper into small
triangular pieces. Heat the oil in a
preheated wok or large frying pan (skillet)
and stir-fry the (bell) pepper for about
1 minute. Add the garlic, ginger, spring
onion (scallion), salt and squid. Continue
stirring for a further minute.

5 Finally, add the black bean sauce and
wine or sherry and blend well. Serve
hot, sprinkled with sesame oil.

To Clean the Squid

*Clean the squid by first cutting off the
head. Cut off the tentacles and reserve.
Remove the small soft bone at the base of
the tentacles and the transparent
backbone, as well as the ink bag. Peel off
the thin skin, then wash and dry well.*

Braised Fish Fillets

SERVES 4

3–4 small Chinese dried mushrooms
300–350 g / 10–12 oz fish fillets
1 tsp salt
½ egg white, lightly beaten
1 tsp cornflour (cornstarch) paste (see
    page 30)
600 ml / 1 pint / 2½ cups vegetable oil
1 tsp finely chopped ginger root
2 spring onions (scallions), chopped finely
1 garlic clove, chopped finely
½ small green (bell) pepper, cored, seeded
    and cut into small cubes
½ small carrot, sliced thinly
60 g / 2 oz canned sliced bamboo shoots,
    rinsed and drained
½ tsp sugar
1 tbsp light soy sauce
1 tsp rice wine or dry sherry
1 tbsp chilli bean sauce
2–3 tbsp Chinese Stock (see page 9)
    or water
a few drops of sesame oil

1 Soak the Chinese mushrooms in warm
water for 30 minutes, then drain on
paper towels, reserving the soaking water
for stock or soup.

2 Squeeze the mushrooms to extract all
the moisture. Cut off and discard any
hard stems and slice the caps thinly.

3 Cut the fish into bite-sized pieces,
then place in a shallow dish and mix
with a pinch of salt, the egg white and the
cornflour (cornstarch) paste, turning the
fish to coat well.

4 Heat the oil in a preheated wok or
large frying pan (skillet) and deep-fry
the fish pieces for about 1 minute.
Remove with a slotted spoon and drain
on paper towels.

5 Pour off the oil, leaving about
1 tablespoon in the wok or frying pan
(skillet). Add the ginger, spring onions
(scallions) and garlic to flavour the oil for
a few seconds, then add the vegetables
and stir-fry for about 1 minute.

6 Add the salt, sugar, soy sauce, wine or
sherry, chilli bean sauce and stock or
water and bring to the boil. Add the fish
pieces, stir to coat well with the sauce, and
braise for another minute. Sprinkle with
sesame oil and serve immediately.

Kung Po Chicken with Cashew Nuts

SERVES 4

250–300 g / 8–10 oz boneless chicken
  meat, skinned
¼ tsp salt
⅓ egg white
1 tsp cornflour (cornstarch) paste (see
  page 30)
1 medium green (bell) pepper, cored and
  seeded
4 tbsp vegetable oil
1 spring onion (scallion), cut into short
  sections
a few small slices ginger root
4–5 small dried red chillies, soaked,
  deseeded and shredded
2 tbsp crushed yellow bean sauce
1 tsp rice wine or dry sherry
125 g / 4 oz / 1 cup roasted cashew nuts
a few drops of sesame oil

1 Cut the chicken into small cubes
  about the size of sugar lumps. Place
the chicken in a small bowl and mix with
a pinch of salt, the egg white and the
cornflour (cornstarch) paste, in that order.

2 Cut the green (bell) pepper into cubes
  or triangles about the same size as the
chicken pieces.

3 Heat the oil in a preheated wok or
  large frying pan (skillet), add the
chicken and stir-fry for about 1 minute, or
until the colour changes. Remove with a
slotted spoon and keep warm.

4 Add the spring onion (scallion),
  ginger, chillies and green (bell) pepper.
Stir-fry for about 1 minute, then add the
chicken with the yellow bean sauce and
wine or sherry. Blend well and stir-fry for a
further minute.

5 Finally, stir in the cashew nuts and
  sesame oil. Serve hot.

Aromatic & Crispy Duck

SERVES 4

2 large duckling quarters
1 tsp salt
3–4 pieces star anise
1 tsp Szechuan peppercorns
1 tsp cloves
2 cinnamon sticks, broken into pieces
2–3 spring onions (scallions), cut into short
    sections
4–5 small slices ginger root
3–4 tbsp rice wine or dry sherry
vegetable oil, for deep-frying

TO SERVE:
12 ready-made pancakes or 12 crisp lettuce
    leaves
hoi-sin or plum sauce
¼ cucumber, shredded thinly
3–4 spring onions (scallions), shredded thinly

1 Rub the duck with the salt and arrange
the star anise, peppercorns, cloves and
cinnamon on top. Sprinkle with the spring
onions (scallions), ginger and wine and
leave to marinate for at least 3–4 hours.

2 Arrange the duck (with the marinade
spices) on a plate that will fit inside a
bamboo steamer. Pour some hot water
into a wok and place the bamboo steamer
in the wok, resting on a trivet. Put in the
duck and cover with the bamboo lid.

3 Steam the duck over high heat for at
least 2–3 hours, until tender and
cooked through. Top up the hot water
from time to time as required.

4 Remove the duck and leave to cool
for at least 4–5 hours (this is very
important, for unless the duck is cold and
dry it will not be crispy).

5 Pour the oil into a preheated wok or
large frying pan (skillet) and heat until
smoking. Fry the duck, skin-side down, for
4–5 minutes or until crisp and brown.
Remove and drain on paper towels.

6 To serve, scrape the meat off the
bone. Place 1 teaspoon of hoi-sin or
plum sauce on the centre of a pancake
(or lettuce leaf) and add a few pieces of
cucumber and spring onion (scallion) and
a portion of duck. Wrap up to form a
small parcel and eat with your fingers.
Provide plenty of napkins for your guests.

Szechuan Chilli Chicken

SERVES 4

500 g / 1 lb chicken thighs
¼ tsp pepper
1 tbsp sugar
2 tsp light soy sauce
1 tsp dark soy sauce
1 tbsp rice wine or dry sherry
2 tsp cornflour (cornstarch)
2–3 tbsp vegetable oil
1–2 garlic cloves, crushed
2 spring onions (scallions), cut into short
    sections, with the green and white parts
    separated
4–6 small dried red chillies, soaked and
    deseeded
2 tbsp crushed yellow bean sauce
about 150 ml / ¼ pint / ⅔ cup Chinese Stock
    (see page 9) or water

1 Cut or chop the chicken thighs into bite-sized pieces and marinate with the pepper, sugar, soy sauce, wine or sherry and cornflour (cornstarch) for 25–30 minutes.

2 Heat the oil in a preheated wok or large frying pan (skillet), add the chicken pieces and stir-fry until lightly brown for about 1–2 minutes. Remove the chicken pieces with a slotted spoon, transfer to a warm dish and reserve.

3 Add the garlic, the white parts of the spring onions (scallions), the chillies and the yellow bean sauce to the wok or frying pan (skillet) and stir-fry for about 30 seconds, blending well.

4 Return the chicken pieces to the wok or frying pan (skillet), stirring constantly for about 1–2 minutes, then add the stock or water, bring to the boil and cover.

5 Braise over medium heat for 5–6 minutes, stirring once or twice. Garnish with the green parts of the spring onions (scallions) and serve immediately.

Fish-flavoured Shredded Pork

SERVES 4

about 2 tbsp dried wood ears
250–300 g / 8–10 oz pork fillet (tenderloin)
1 tsp salt
2 tsp cornflour (cornstarch) paste (see
    page 30)
3 tbsp vegetable oil
1 garlic clove, chopped finely
½ tsp finely chopped ginger root
2 spring onions (scallions), chopped finely,
    with the white and green parts separated
2 celery stalks, sliced thinly
½ tsp sugar
1 tbsp light soy sauce
1 tbsp chilli bean sauce
2 tsp rice vinegar
1 tsp rice wine or dry sherry
a few drops of sesame oil

1 Soak the wood ears in warm water for
about 20 minutes, then rinse in cold
water until the water is clear. Drain well,
then cut into thin shreds.

2 Cut the pork into thin shreds, then
mix in a bowl with a pinch of salt and
about half the cornflour (cornstarch)
paste until well coated.

3 Heat 1 tablespoon of oil in a
preheated wok or large frying pan
(skillet). Add the pork strips and stir-fry
for 1 minute, or until the colour changes,
then remove with a slotted spoon.

4 Add the remaining oil to the wok or
frying pan (skillet) and heat. Add the
garlic, ginger, the white parts of the spring
onions (scallions), the wood ears and
celery. Stir-fry for about 1 minute, then
return the pork strips together with the
salt, sugar, soy sauce, chili bean sauce,
vinegar and wine or sherry. Blend well and
continue stirring for a further minute.

5 Finally add the green parts of the
spring onions (scallions) and blend in
the remaining cornflour (cornstarch)
paste and the sesame oil. Stir until the
sauce has thickened and serve hot.

DRIED WOOD EARS

Also known as cloud ears, these dried
grey-black fungi are always soaked in
warm water before using. They have a
crunchy texture and a mild flavour.

Beef & Chilli Black Bean Sauce

SERVES 4

250–300 g / 8–10 oz beef steak such
   as rump
1 small onion
1 small green (bell) pepper, cored and
   deseeded
about 300 ml / ½ pint / 1¼ cups
   vegetable oil
1 spring onion (scallion), cut into short
   sections
a few small slices ginger root
1–2 small green or red chillies, seeded and
   sliced, or ¼–½ tsp chilli powder
2 tbsp crushed black bean sauce

MARINADE:
½ tsp bicarbonate of soda or baking powder
½ tsp sugar
1 tbsp light soy sauce
2 tsp rice wine or dry sherry
2 tsp cornflour (cornstarch) paste (see
   page 30)
2 tsp sesame oil

1 Cut the beef into small thin strips. Mix together the marinade ingredients in a shallow dish, add the beef strips, turn to coat and leave to marinate for at least 2–3 hours – the longer the better.

2 Cut the onion and green (bell) pepper into small cubes.

3 Heat the oil in a preheated wok or large frying pan (skillet). Add the beef strips and stir-fry for about 1 minute, or until the colour changes. Remove with a slotted spoon and drain on paper towels. Keep warm.

4 Pour off the excess oil, leaving about 1 tablespoon in the wok or frying pan (skillet). Add the spring onion (scallion), ginger, chillies or chilli powder, onion and green (bell) pepper and stir-fry for about 1 minute. Add the black bean sauce, stir until smooth then return the beef strips to the wok or frying pan (skillet). Blend well and stir-fry for another minute. Serve hot.

Oyster Sauce Beef

SERVES 4

300 g / 10 oz beef steak
1 tsp sugar
1 tbsp light soy sauce
1 tsp rice wine or dry sherry
1 tsp cornflour (cornstarch) paste (see
page 30)
½ small carrot
60 g / 2 oz mangetout (snow peas)
60 g / 2 oz canned bamboo shoots, rinsed
and drained
60 g / 2 oz canned straw mushrooms,
rinsed and drained
about 300 ml / ½ pint / 1¼ cups
vegetable oil
1 spring onion (scallion), cut into short
sections
2–3 small slices ginger root
½ tsp salt
2 tbsp oyster sauce
2–3 tbsp Chinese Stock (see page 9)
or water

1 Cut the beef into small, thin slices. Place in a shallow dish with the sugar, soy sauce, wine or sherry and cornflour (cornstarch) paste and leave to marinate for 25–30 minutes.

2 Slice the carrot, mangetout (snow peas), bamboo shoots and straw mushrooms so that as far as possible the vegetable pieces are of uniform size.

3 Heat the oil in a preheated wok or large frying pan (skillet). Add the beef slices and stir-fry for about 1 minute, then remove with a slotted spoon and keep warm.

4 Pour off the oil, leaving about 1 tablespoon in the wok or frying pan (skillet). Add the sliced vegetables with the spring onion (scallion) and ginger and stir-fry for about 2 minutes. Add the salt, beef, oyster sauce and stock or water. Blend well until heated through, and serve with a dip sauce, if liked.

Stir-fried Seasonal Vegetables

SERVES 4

1 medium red (bell) pepper, cored
   and seeded
125 g / 4 oz courgettes (zucchini)
125 g / 4 oz cauliflower
125 g / 4 oz French beans
3 tbsp vegetable oil
a few small slices ginger root
½ tsp salt
½ tsp sugar
Chinese Stock (see page 9) or water
1 tbsp light soy sauce
a few drops of sesame oil (optional)

1 Cut the red (bell) pepper into small squares. Thinly slice the courgettes (zucchini). Trim the cauliflower and divide into small florets, discarding any thick stalks. Make sure the vegetables are cut into roughly similar shapes and sizes to allow even cooking.

2 Top and tail the French beans, then cut them in half.

3 Heat the oil in a preheated wok or large frying pan (skillet), add the vegetables and stir-fry with the ginger for about 2 minutes.

4 Add the salt and sugar to the wok or frying pan (skillet) and continue to stir-fry for 1–2 minutes, adding a little Chinese stock or water if the vegetables appear to be too dry. Do not add liquid unless it seems necessary.

5 Add the soy sauce and sesame oil (if using), blend well to coat the vegetables lightly and serve immediately.

VEGETABLES

Almost any vegetables could be used in this dish: other good choices would be mangetout (snow peas), broccoli florets, carrots, baby corn cobs, green peas, Chinese cabbage and young spinach leaves. Either white or black (oyster) mushrooms can also be used to give a greater diversity of textures. Make sure there is a good variety of colour, and always include several crisp vegetables.

Braised Chinese Leaves

SERVES 4

500 g / 1 lb Chinese leaves or firm-packed
    white cabbage
3 tbsp vegetable oil
½ tsp Szechuan peppercorns
5–6 small dried red chillies, seeded and
    chopped, or ½–¾ tsp chilli powder
½ tsp salt
1 tbsp sugar
1 tbsp light soy sauce
1 tbsp rice vinegar
a few drops of sesame oil (optional)

1 Shred the Chinese leaves or cabbage
crosswise into thin pieces. (If using
cabbage, cut out the thick core with a
sharp knife before shredding.)

2 Heat the oil in a preheated wok or
large frying pan (skillet), add the
Szechuan peppercorns and chillies or
chilli powder and stir for a few seconds.

3 Add the shredded Chinese leaves or
cabbage, stir-fry for about 1 minute,
then add salt and continue stirring for a
further minute.

4 Add the sugar, soy sauce and vinegar,
blend well and braise for a further
minute. Finally sprinkle on the sesame oil,
if using. Serve hot or cold.

SZECHUAN PEPPERCORNS

*It is important to use the correct type of
peppercorns in preparing this dish.
Szechuan red peppercorns are not true
peppercorns, but reddish-brown dried
berries with a pungent, aromatic odour
which distinguishes them from the hotter
black peppercorns. Roast them briefly
in the oven or sauté them in a dry frying
pan (skillet).*

Money Bags

SERVES 4

3 Chinese dried mushrooms (if unavailable,
   use thinly sliced open-cup mushrooms)
250 g / 8 oz / 2 cups plain (all-purpose)
   flour
1 egg, beaten
75 ml / 2½ fl oz / 5 tbsp water
1 tsp baking powder
¾ tsp salt
2 tbsp vegetable oil
2 spring onions (scallions), chopped
90 g / 3 oz / ½ cup sweetcorn (corn) kernels
½ red chilli, deseeded and chopped
1 tbsp brown bean sauce

1 Place the dried mushrooms in a small
   bowl, cover with warm water and
leave to soak for 20–25 minutes.

2 To make the wrappers, sift the flour
   into a bowl. Add the egg and mix in
lightly. Stir in the water, baking powder
and salt. Mix to make a soft dough and
knead lightly on a floured board until
smooth. Cover with a damp cloth and set
aside for 5–6 minutes. This allows the
baking powder time to activate so that the
dumplings swell when steaming.

3 Drain the mushrooms, squeezing
   them dry. Remove the tough centres
and chop the caps.

4 Heat the oil in a preheated wok or
   large frying pan (skillet). Add the
mushrooms, spring onions (scallions),
sweetcorn (corn) and chilli and stir-fry for
2 minutes. Stir in the brown bean sauce
and remove from the heat.

5 Roll the dough into a large sausage
   and cut into 24 even-sized pieces. Roll
each piece out into a thin round and
place a teaspoonful of the filling in the
centre. Gather up the edges to a point,
pinch together and twist to seal.

6 Stand the dumplings in an oiled
   steaming basket. Place over a
saucepan of simmering water, cover and
steam for 12–14 minutes before serving.

Carrots & Parsnips
with Coconut

SERVES 2

90 g / 3 oz / ⅓ cup creamed coconut
300 ml / ½ pint / 1¼ cups hot water
15 g / ½ oz / 2 tbsp flaked (slivered)
   almonds
4 tbsp vegetable oil
5 cardamom pods
4 thin slices ginger root
350 g / 12 oz / 2½ cups carrots, sliced
350 g / 12 oz / 2½ cups parsnips, cored and
   cut into small chunks
¼ tsp five-spice powder
15 g / ½ oz / 2 tbsp ground almonds
200 g / 7 oz / 4 cups young spinach leaves
½ red onion, sliced thinly
1 garlic clove, sliced
salt

1 Crumble the creamed coconut into a
bowl or jug, add the hot water and stir
until dissolved.

2 Heat a saucepan and dry-fry the
flaked (slivered) almonds until golden.
Remove and set aside.

3 Heat half the oil in the pan and add
the cardamom and ginger. Fry for 30
seconds to flavour the oil. Add the carrots
and parsnips. Stir-fry for 2–3 minutes.

4 Stir in the five-spice powder and
ground almonds and pour in the
coconut liquid. Bring to the boil and
season with salt to taste. Cover and
simmer for 12–15 minutes until the
vegetables are tender. Stir occasionally,
adding extra water if necessary.

5 Wash the spinach, drain it well and
remove any stalks. Heat the remaining
oil in a preheated wok or large frying pan
(skillet). Add the onion and garlic and
stir-fry for 2 minutes. Add the spinach
and stir-fry until it has just wilted. Drain
off any excess liquid. Season with salt.

6 Remove the cardamom and ginger
from the carrots and parsnips and
adjust the seasoning to taste. Serve on a
bed of the spinach, sprinkled with the
flaked (slivered) almonds.

Chicken or Pork Chow Mein

SERVES 4

250 g / 8 oz egg noodles
5 tbsp vegetable oil
250 g / 8 oz chicken breast meat or pork
    fillet (tenderloin), cooked
125 g / 4 oz French beans
2 tbsp light soy sauce
1 tsp salt
½ tsp sugar
1 tbsp Chinese rice wine or dry sherry
2 spring onions (scallions), shredded finely
a little Chinese stock (see page 9)
a few drops of sesame oil
chilli sauce to serve (optional)

1 Cook the noodles in boiling water
  according to the instructions on the
packet, then drain and rinse under cold
water. Drain again then toss with
1 tablespoon of the oil.

2 Slice the meat into thin shreds and
  top and tail the beans.

3 Heat 3 tablespoons of oil in a
  preheated wok or large frying pan
(skillet) until hot, add the noodles and
stir-fry for 2–3 minutes with 1 tablespoon
soy sauce, then remove to a serving dish.
Keep warm.

4 Heat the remaining oil and stir-fry the
  beans and meat for about 2 minutes.
Add the salt, sugar, wine or sherry, the
remaining soy sauce and about half the
spring onions (scallions) to the wok or
frying pan (skillet).

5 Blend the meat mixture well and add
  a little stock if necessary, then pour on
top of the noodles. Sprinkle with sesame
oil and the remaining spring onions
(scallions). Serve hot or cold with or
without chilli sauce.

Fragrant Steamed Rice in Lotus Leaves

SERVES 4

2 lotus leaves

4 Chinese dried mushrooms (if unavailable, use thinly sliced open-cup mushrooms)

175 g / 6 oz / generous ¾ cup long-grain rice

1 cinnamon stick

6 cardamom pods

4 cloves

1 tsp salt

1 tbsp vegetable oil

2 eggs, beaten lightly

2 spring onions (scallions), chopped

1 tbsp light soy sauce

2 tbsp dry sherry

1 tsp sugar

1 tsp sesame oil

1 Unfold the lotus leaves and cut along the fold to divide each leaf in half. Lay on a large baking tray and pour over hot water to cover. Leave to soak for about 30 minutes or until the leaves have softened.

2 Place the dried mushrooms in a small bowl and cover with warm water. Leave to soak for 20–25 minutes.

3 Cook the rice in plenty of boiling water in a saucepan with the cinnamon stick, cardamom pods, cloves and salt for about 10 minutes – the rice should be partially cooked. Drain well and remove the cinnamon stick.

4 Heat the oil in a preheated wok or frying pan (skillet). Cook the eggs quickly, stirring constantly, until set then remove and set aside.

5 Drain the mushrooms and squeeze out excess water. Remove the tough centres and chop the caps. Place the rice in a bowl. Stir in the mushrooms, egg, spring onions (scallions), soy sauce, sherry, sugar and sesame oil. Season with salt to taste.

6 Drain the lotus leaves and divide the rice mixture into 4 portions. Place a portion in the centre of each leaf and fold up. Place in a steamer, cover and steam over simmering water for 20 minutes. To serve, cut the tops of the lotus leaves open to expose the fragrant rice inside.

Spicy Coconut Rice with Green Lentils

SERVES 2–4

90 g / 3 oz / ⅓ cup green lentils
250 g / 8 oz / generous 1 cup long-grain rice
2 tbsp vegetable oil
1 onion, sliced
2 garlic cloves, crushed
3 curry leaves
1 stalk lemon grass, chopped (if unavailable,
*   use grated rind of ½ lemon)*
1 green chilli, deseeded and chopped
½ tsp cumin seeds
1½ tsp salt
90 g / 3 oz / ⅓ cup creamed coconut
600 ml / 1 pint / 2½ cups hot water
2 tbsp chopped fresh coriander (cilantro)

TO GARNISH:
sprigs of coriander (cilantro)
shredded radishes
shredded cucumber

1 Wash the lentils and place in a saucepan. Cover with cold water, bring to the boil and boil rapidly for 10 minutes. Wash the rice thoroughly and drain well.

2 Heat the oil in a large saucepan which has a tight-fitting lid and fry the onion for 3–4 minutes. Add the garlic, curry leaves, lemon grass, chilli, cumin seeds and salt, and stir well.

3 Drain the lentils and rinse. Add to the onion and spices with the rice and mix well. Add the creamed coconut to the hot water and stir until dissolved. Stir into the rice mixture and bring to the boil. Turn down the heat to low, put the lid on tightly and leave to cook undisturbed for 15 minutes.

4 Without removing the lid, take the pan from the heat and leave to rest for 10 minutes to allow the rice and lentils to finish cooking in their own steam.

5 Stir in the chopped coriander (cilantro) and remove the curry leaves. Serve garnished with sprigs of coriander (cilantro) and shredded radishes and cucumber.

Singapore-style Rice Noodles

SERVES 4

200 g / 7 oz rice noodles
125 g / 4 oz cooked chicken or pork
60 g / 2 oz peeled prawns (shrimp),
  defrosted if frozen
4 tbsp vegetable oil
1 medium onion, shredded thinly
125 g / 4 oz / 2 cups fresh bean-sprouts
1 tsp salt
1 tbsp mild curry powder
2 tbsp light soy sauce
2 spring onions (scallions), shredded thinly
1–2 small fresh green or red chillies, seeded
  and shredded thinly

1 Soak the rice noodles in boiling water for 8–10 minutes, then rinse in cold water and drain well.

2 Thinly slice the cooked meat. Dry the prawns (shrimp) on paper towels.

3 Heat the oil in a preheated wok or large frying pan (skillet). Add the onion and stir-fry until opaque. Add the bean-sprouts and stir-fry for 1 minute.

4 Add the noodles with the meat and prawns (shrimp), and continue stirring for a further minute.

5 Blend in the salt, curry powder and soy sauce, followed by the spring onions (scallions) and chillies. Stir-fry for a further minute, then serve immediately.

RICE NOODLES

Rice noodles are very delicate noodles made from rice flour. They become soft and pliable after being soaked for about 10 minutes. If you wish to store them after they have been soaked, toss them in a few drops of sesame oil then place them in a sealed container in the refrigerator.

VARIATION

For a really authentic flavour include 1 tablespoon dried shrimps, which are available from oriental food stores and have a strong, pungent taste. Soak in warm water for 30 minutes, drain and add to the noodles at step 4.

Index